ALABAMA

KATHY FEENEY

Consultants

MELISSA N. MATUSEVICH, PH.D.

Curriculum and Instruction Specialist
Blacksburg, Virginia

LOU ELLEN NICHOLS
Youth Services Librarian
Gardendale-Martha Moore Public Library
Gardendale, Alabama

CHILDREN'S PRESS®

AN IMPRINT OF SCHOLASTIC INC.

New York • Toronto • London • Auckland • Sydney • Mexico City
New Delhi • Hong Kong • Danbury, Connecticut

Alabama is in the southeastern part of the United States. It is bordered by Georgia, Florida, Tennessee, Mississippi, and the Gulf of Mexico.

Project Editor: Meredith DeSousa
Art Director: Marie O'Neill
Photo Researcher: Marybeth Kavanagh
Design: Robin West, Ox and Company, Inc.
Page 6 map and recipe art: Susan Hunt Yule
All other maps: XNR Productions, Inc.

Library of Congress Cataloging-in-Publication Data

Feeney, Kathy, 1954–
      Alabama / by Kathy Feeney.
        p. cm. – (From sea to shining sea)
      Includes biographical references and index.
  ISBN-13: 978-0-531-20800-7
  ISBN-10: 0-531-20800-1
    1. Alabama—Juvenile literature. I. Title. II. Series.

F326.3 .F44 2008
976.1—dc22   2007046543

TABLE of CONTENTS

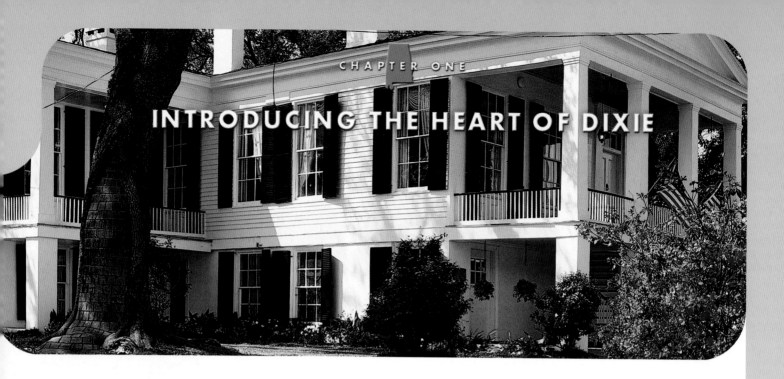

CHAPTER ONE

INTRODUCING THE HEART OF DIXIE

Part of Alabama's rich history includes magnificent plantations such as Oakleigh mansion, built in 1833 in Mobile.

In many ways, the story of Alabama is also the story of the United States. Alabama has given us traditional American music, world-class athletes, and courageous role models. Many of our country's "firsts" came from Alabama, too. George Washington Carver invented peanut butter at the Tuskegee Institute, and Wilbur and Orville Wright established the world's first flying school in Montgomery. At George C. Marshall Space Flight Center in Huntsville, scientists created the *Saturn V* rocket that carried the first men to the moon.

The state's history also reminds us of America's more difficult times. Like many southern states, Alabama was once home to slavery and racial injustice. During the 1950s and 1960s, Alabama was a place where ordinary people became heroes, risking their lives for the cause of civil rights. African Americans fought for the right to attend school, eat in restaurants, and vote. Today, visitors can still see the plantations and cotton fields where enslaved Africans labored.

Alabama is a land of breezy beaches, majestic mountains, fairy-tale forests, and grand gardens. It is a place where people drink iced tea and lemonade on porch swings, and seek shelter from the humid summer heat in hammocks. Harper Lee, an Alabama native and author of the Pulitzer Prize–winning novel *To Kill a Mockingbird*, described a typical summer day in the 1930s. "Men's stiff collars wilted by nine in the morning," Lee wrote. "Ladies bathed before noon, after three o'clock naps, and by nightfall were like soft teacakes with frosting of sweat and sweet talcum."

Alabama is sometimes called the Heart of Dixie. The name "Dixie" originated in the mid-1800s. After a bank in Louisiana issued $10 bills engraved with the word "dix," (the French word for ten), the South became known as Dixieland. Alabama was called the Heart of Dixie because Montgomery served as the first capital of the Confederacy, an alliance of the southern states, during the Civil War.

What comes to mind when you think of Alabama?

❖ Graceful magnolia trees, stately pines, and sweet-smelling camellias
❖ Groves of pecan trees
❖ Southern foods such as black-eyed peas and collard greens
❖ Jazz music inspired by the spiritual songs of slaves
❖ Huge plantations and fields of cotton
❖ Rosa Parks refusing to give up her seat on a Montgomery bus
❖ Civil rights leader Martin Luther King Jr. and his followers marching from Selma to Montgomery

Alabama means many things to many people. In this book, you'll read about some of the people and events that have shaped the Heart of Dixie. You'll discover the story of Alabama.

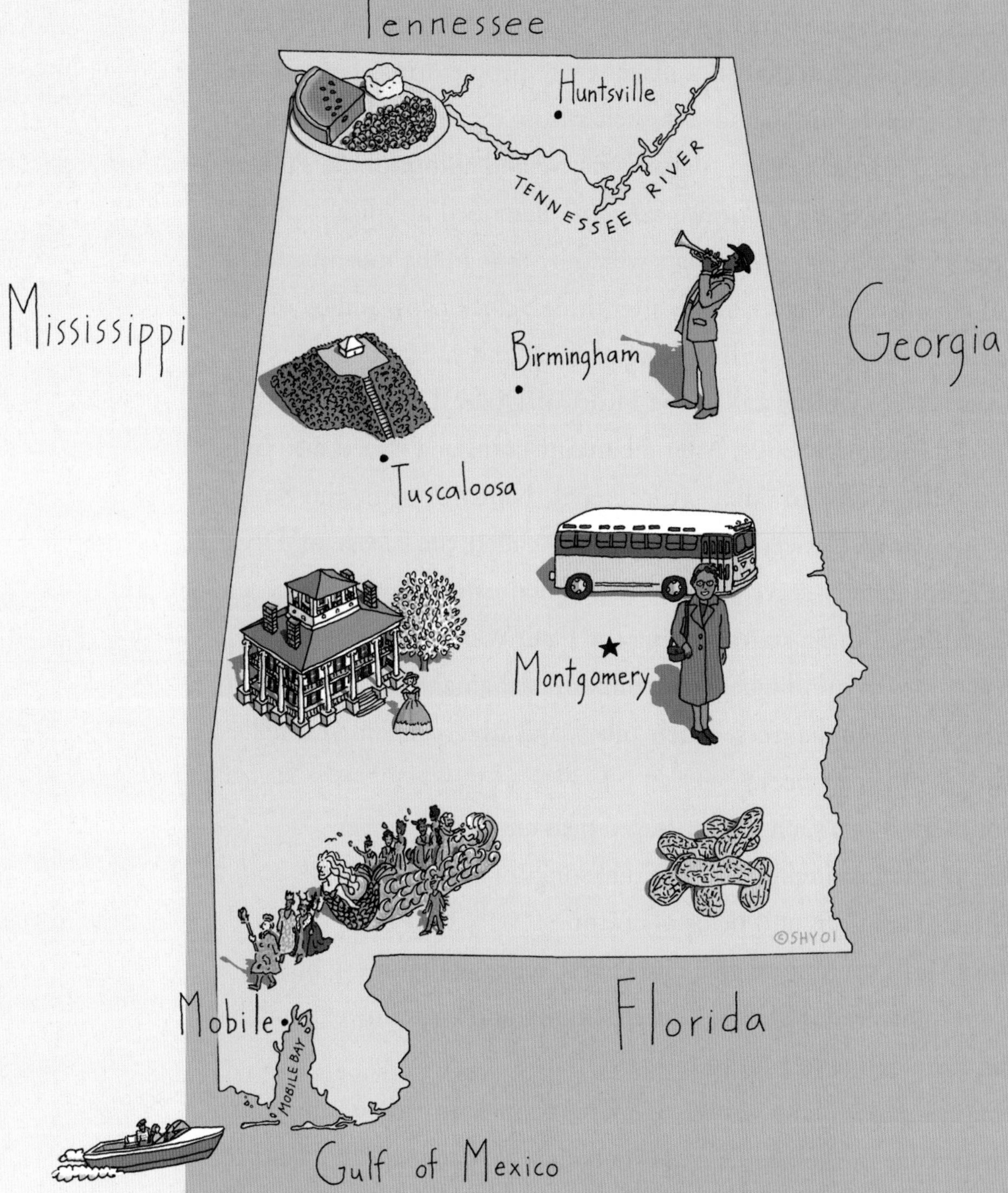

Tennessee

Huntsville

TENNESSEE RIVER

Mississippi

Birmingham

Georgia

Tuscaloosa

Montgomery

©SHY01

Mobile

MOBILE BAY

Florida

Gulf of Mexico

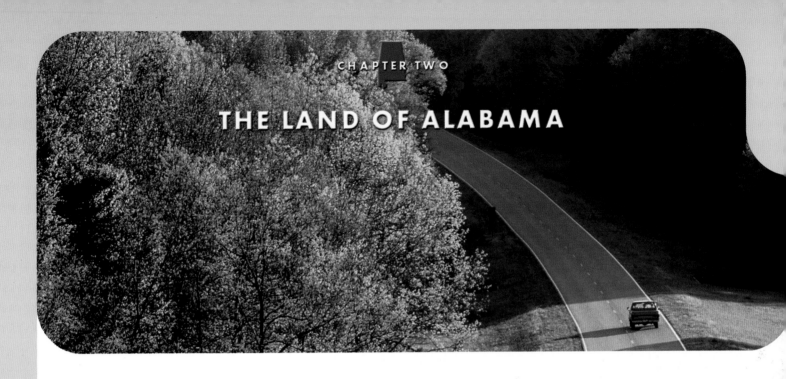

CHAPTER TWO

THE LAND OF ALABAMA

Alabama is in the southeastern United States in a region called the Deep South. If you look at a map, you'll see that Alabama is shaped almost like a rectangle with a narrow section on the bottom left that resembles a foot sticking out. To the north lies Tennessee, and to the south lie Florida and the Gulf of Mexico. Georgia is to the east, and Mississippi is to the west.

You can travel from Alabama to one of these neighboring states in just a few hours. With 52,419 square miles (135,765 square kilometers) of land, Alabama is a medium-size state. It is the 30th-largest state in the country.

Motorists enjoy the scenic views from Natchez Trace Parkway in the northwestern corner of Alabama.

GEOGRAPHIC REGIONS

The land of Alabama stretches across prairies and beaches, down into valleys, high into mountains, and deep into forests. There are six land

Alabama's Gulf Coast boasts sandy beaches and a moderate climate.

regions in Alabama: the East Gulf Coastal Plain, the Black Belt, the Piedmont Plateau, the Appalachian Ridge and Valley, the Cumberland Plateau, and the Interior Low Plateau.

East Gulf Coastal Plain

The East Gulf Coastal Plain covers about three-quarters of southern and northwestern Alabama, making it the state's largest land region. There are several sections within the East Gulf Coastal Plain, including the Mobile River Delta, the Wiregrass, the Gulf Coast, and the Central Pine Belt.

The Mobile River Delta is in the southwestern part of the plain. The Mobile River is the fourth-largest river system in the United States. The Mobile River Delta, where the river deposits sediment (mud, sand, and gravel) as it enters the Gulf of Mexico, is the largest delta section in the United States. Alligators and other animals inhabit the low, swampy land in this region. Most of southern Alabama is less than 500 feet (152 meters) above sea level.

A section called the Wiregrass covers the southeast. Its name comes from a wiry grass that once covered this region. Today this area is used mostly for farmland, including cotton fields.

The stretch of land between Mobile Bay and Perdido Bay is called the Gulf Coast. Alabama's coastline stretches 53 miles (85 km) along the Gulf of Mexico. It starts at the Mississippi border and ends at Perdido River on the Florida border. Dauphin Island is a barrier island in the Gulf of Mexico, about 33 miles (53 km) from Mobile. In 2000 it was estimated that about 2,000 people live on the island year-round. Dauphin Island is sometimes called the "crown jewel of the Gulf Coast" because of its beautiful scenery and rich history.

The northern region of the plain, called the Central Pine Belt, borders the Appalachian highlands. This hilly region has an abundance of pine forests and is home to Alabama's lumber industry.

Most cotton production in Alabama is done in the southeast.

FIND OUT MORE

Forests cover more than two-thirds of Alabama, or nearly 22 million acres—about the size of Indiana. Red cedar, cypress, sweet gum, black walnut, hemlock, hickory, oak, poplar, and Southern pine are just a few of the trees that grow in Alabama. How has this wealth of forests helped Alabama to develop throughout its history?

Black Belt

The Black Belt is a narrow strip of prairie land about 25 to 50 miles (40 to 80 km) wide. Squeezed between the northern and southern sections of the East Gulf Coastal Plain, it was named for its shape (which looks like a belt) and its fertile black clay soil.

Early Alabamians liked this land of broad plains because of its rich soil, woodlands, and rivers. Many farmers built cotton plantations here until an insect called the boll weevil damaged cotton crops in the early 1900s. As a result of the damage, many of the area's farmers began to plant soybeans and raise cattle. Today some of Alabama's largest cities are located in the Black Belt, including Cahaba, Montgomery, Selma, and Tuscaloosa.

Piedmont Plateau

The Piedmont Plateau is in east central Alabama. This region's hills, ridges, and valleys are rich with coal, iron, marble, and limestone deposits. It is also home to the state's highest point, Cheaha Mountain, which rises 2,407 feet (734 m). At Cheaha State Park, visitors can hike, swim, and enjoy spectacular mountain views.

Appalachian Ridge and Valley

The Appalachian Ridge and Valley is north of the Piedmont Plateau. This region has valleys, or depressions in the earth's surface, surrounded by steep cliffs. It also has an abundance of coal, iron ore, and limestone, which led to the development of Birmingham, a center of Alabama's steel industry located in Jones Valley.

Scenic waterfalls are one of the highlights of DeSoto State Park, located in the Appalachian Ridge and Valley Region.

FIND OUT MORE

Because soil in the Appalachian Plateau is sandy, farmers in this region must use fertilizer in order to grow crops there. What is the best kind of soil for growing crops?

The land in northwestern Alabama is excellent for farming.

Cumberland Plateau

The Cumberland Plateau, located north of the Appalachian Ridge and Valley, stretches from Alabama's hilly northeastern corner to the center of the state. This region is also known as the Appalachian Plateau because of its location within the Appalachian Mountain range. The Cumberland Plateau is the southwestern division of the Appalachian Mountains, which extend down the eastern part of North America from Quebec, Canada to northern Alabama.

Early settlers discovered that the sandy soil of the Cumberland Plateau was not good for growing crops. Today, farmers in this area use fertilizer to feed the soil so that they can grow cotton, hay, and vegetables. They also raise hogs and poultry on the Cumberland Plateau.

Interior Low Plateau

Northwestern Alabama is called the Interior Low Plateau. This section spans the Tennessee River Valley. The land here is fertile and excellent for growing corn, cotton, and hay.

One of the highlights of this region is Dismals Canyon, designated a National Natural Landmark in 1974. Hidden in the foothills of the Appalachian

Mountains, the canyon was inhabited nearly 10,000 years ago by Native American tribes. There are more than 350 species of plants and trees there as well as cliffs, boulders, natural bridges, and waterfalls. Visitors can camp, hike, swim, and canoe at Dismals Canyon.

RIVERS AND LAKES

With twenty-six rivers covering more than 1,600 miles (2,575 km), almost every part of Alabama has a river. In fact, Alabama has 1,438 miles (2,314 km) of navigable channels—more than any other state. Rivers and lakes have always been an important part of the state's development. They provided a place for early Alabamians to settle and establish trade ports. Today, dams are built on rivers to produce electricity for the people who live in Alabama.

The most important river system in Alabama is the Mobile River system, which flows south into Mobile Bay and the Gulf of Mexico. The Mobile River is formed by the merging of the Tombigbee and Alabama Rivers, about 45 miles (72 km) north of Mobile.

The Alabama and the Tombigbee are the state's longest rivers. The Alabama River is more than 310 miles (499 km) long and begins north of Montgomery. Its tributaries are the Cahaba, Coosa, and Tallapoosa Rivers. The Tombigbee, which is about 400 miles (644 kilometers)

The Mobile River provides transportation for coal, wood products, and other cargo.

EXTRA! EXTRA!

The Alabama River was named for a Native American tribe called *Alabama* or *Alibamon*, who inhabited the land when European explorers arrived. The name Alabama is said to be a combination of two Choctaw words: *alba*, which means "vegetation," and *amo*, which means "to gather." Together the words mean "vegetation gatherers."

long, flows southeast from Mississippi into Alabama. The Tennessee River flows west across the northern part of the state. It is the most important river in northern Alabama.

There are no large natural lakes in the state. Most of Alabama's lakes are manmade lakes that have been created by river dams. The largest is Guntersville Lake, spanning 110 square miles (285 sq km). It is formed by the Guntersville Dam on the Tennessee River. Other large lakes include Lake Eufaula on the Chattahoochee River; the Pickwick,

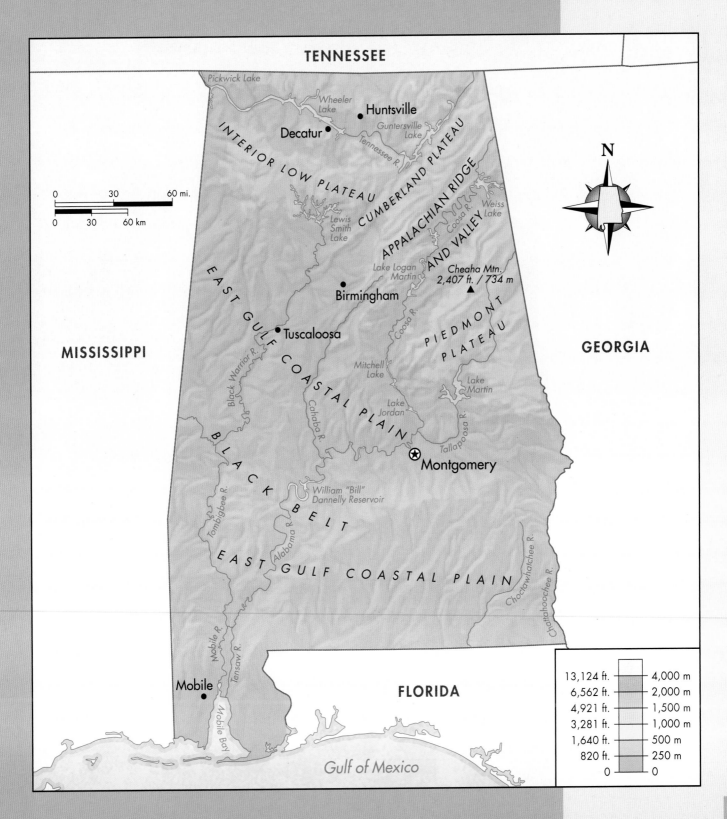

TENNESSEE

Pickwick Lake

Wheeler
Lake

• Huntsville

Decatur •

Guntersville
Lake

Tennessee R.

INTERIOR LOW PLATEAU

CUMBERLAND PLATEAU

APPALACHIAN RIDGE

AND VALLEY

Coosa R.

Weiss
Lake

Lewis
Smith
Lake

Lake Logan
Martin

Cheaha Mtn.
2,407 ft. / 734 m ▲

• Birmingham

Coosa R.

PIEDMONT
PLATEAU

EAST GULF COASTAL PLAIN

• Tuscaloosa

Black Warrior R.

MISSISSIPPI

Cahaba R.

Mitchell
Lake

Lake
Martin

GEORGIA

Lake
Jordan

Tallapoosa R.

⊛ Montgomery

B L A C K

William "Bill"
Dannelly Reservoir

B E L T

Tombigbee R.

Alabama R.

E A S T   G U L F   C O A S T A L   P L A I N

Choctawhatchee R.

Chattahoochee R.

Mobile R.

Mobile •

Tensaw R.

FLORIDA

Mobile Bay

Gulf of Mexico

N

0   30   60 mi.

0   30   60 km

13,124 ft.	4,000 m
6,562 ft.	2,000 m
4,921 ft.	1,500 m
3,281 ft.	1,000 m
1,640 ft.	500 m
820 ft.	250 m
0	0

EXTRA! EXTRA!

One of Alabama's most unique natural features is Little River in northeastern Alabama. It is the only river in the country that flows almost entirely across the top of a mountain. The mountain it flows across is called Lookout Mountain.

Wheeler, and Wilson Lakes on the Tennessee River; Lake Martin on the Tallapoosa River; and Weiss Lake on the Coosa River.

Alabama's lakes are popular with fishermen, swimmers, and boaters. Wheeler National Wildlife Refuge at Wheeler Lake is home to thousands of birds that migrate there in the winter, including blue, Canada, and snow geese.

WILDLIFE

Alabama is home to a variety of wildlife, including bobcats, deer, foxes, rabbits, raccoons, skunks, squirrels, and wild turkeys. Beavers live in colonies in the swamps and the lowlands, and alligators are found in Alabama's southern swamps. Water birds such as ducks and geese live in Alabama during the winter and migrate north every spring. The state also has an abundance of freshwater fish including bass, catfish, and shad. Its coastline is home to saltwater varieties such as flounder, mullet, red snapper, and tarpon, as well as shellfish such as crabs, oysters, and shrimp.

Many gray foxes live in southern Alabama's pine forests.

CLIMATE

Alabama has hot and humid summers and a fairly mild winter climate. Summer temperatures average around 84° Fahrenheit (29° Celsius) throughout most of the state. The highest temperature ever recorded in Alabama was 112°F (44°C) at Centreville on September 5, 1925.

Temperatures in northern Alabama sometimes dip low enough for snow, but the southern coastal plain area is generally warm and subtropical. Winter temperatures are usually about 52°F (11°C). The coldest

FIND OUT MORE

Northern Alabama sometimes receives snow. What weather conditions are necessary for snow to fall? Find out if the southern cities of Miami, Florida, and New Orleans, Louisiana, receive winter temperatures cold enough to create snowfall.

temperature ever recorded in Alabama was a chilly –27°F (–33°C) at New Market on January 30, 1966.

Alabama's annual rainfall averages about 53 inches (135 centimeters), with most of that rain during the summer. Sometimes Alabama's Gulf Coast is hit by hurricanes, or dangerous windstorms that start in the Caribbean Sea or the Atlantic Ocean. (*Hurricane* is a Caribbean Indian word meaning "evil spirit and big wind.") A hurricane has winds of at least 74 miles (119 km) per hour. Hurricanes that hit Alabama usually travel up the Gulf of Mexico. In 1979, Hurricane David struck Alabama and Mississippi, killing eight people and causing billions of dollars in property damage.

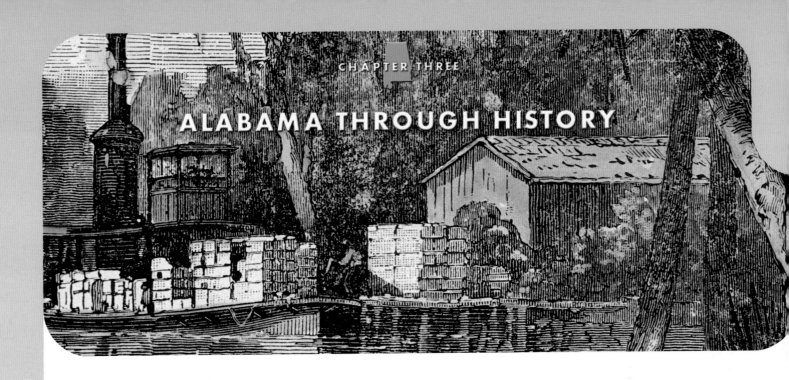

CHAPTER THREE

ALABAMA THROUGH HISTORY

People have lived in Alabama for more than 10,000 years. The first people, called Paleo-Indians (which means "early native people"), came to North America from Asia. At that time, the two continents were connected by land. These ancient people lived in small groups in limestone caves. The caves provided a cool shelter in summer and protection from the cold of winter.

For food, Paleo-Indians gathered wild fruits, roots, and nuts from mountain cliffs. They caught and ate fish, turtles, and mussels from the nearby Tennessee River. They hunted bear and deer for meat and used the hides to make blankets, clothing, and shoes. Animal bones were used to create fishing hooks

During the 1800s, the Port of Mobile served as a major seaport for shipping out cotton.

EXTRA! EXTRA!

Signs of Alabama's earliest people have been found in Dust Cave in northwestern Alabama. The cave was inhabited by Paleo-Indians between 10,500 and 5,200 years ago. Bone tools and stone ornaments that belonged to these early people were preserved in the cave's many layers of sediment. The tools were so well preserved that scientists consider Dust Cave to be one of the most important archaeological sites in the Southeast.

FIND OUT MORE

Scientists who uncover artifacts, or manmade objects from ancient times, are called archaeologists. To avoid damaging an artifact, archaeologists must be very careful when digging up a historic site. Find out what kind of tools archaeologists use to help them uncover ancient artifacts.

Moundville, once the largest city in North America, contained more than 20 earthen mounds.

and sewing needles, and knives and spear tips were made from sharpened stones. Bowls and spoons were made out of turtle shells, and bear teeth became jewelry. Scientists have uncovered many of these items in Russell Cave near Bridgeport in northern Alabama, and Dust Cave in northwestern Alabama.

About A.D. 1,000, descendants of these early residents, called the Woodland Culture, began to gather in villages. These people are sometimes called Mound Builders because they created large mounds of earth in their villages—some as tall as a six-story building. The Woodland people built homes and temples on some mounds, while others were used as burial sites. The Mound Builders mysteriously disappeared in the early seventeenth century.

After the Woodland people, two Native American groups settled in the Alabama region. One group was called the Muskogee, which included the Creek, the Chickasaw, and the Choctaw Indian nations. The Muskogee lived in thatched huts. They settled in one place and built permanent dwellings. They grew crops and raised livestock such as cows, pigs, and horses. A chief and an assistant chief governed the Muskogee. In the 1500s, they were the largest and strongest tribe in the Southeast. By the 1600s, they lived mostly in the area that is today called Alabama. Later they moved west to Oklahoma.

A second group, called the Cherokee, grew beans, corn, and squash. They also hunted animals for food and gathered plants and fruit. Like the Muskogee, they lived in thatched huts arranged in villages. Residents of each Cherokee village lived independently from other villages. They gathered only for special ceremonies or to fight together in times of war.

The Muskogee Creek people were some of Alabama's earliest inhabitants. They lived in small settlements called Creek towns.

EUROPEAN EXPLORERS ARRIVE

In 1519, Spanish explorer Alonso Alvarez de Pineda sailed into Mobile Bay. He was followed by Spaniards Pánfilo de Narváez in 1528 and Hernando de Soto in 1540. These Spaniards came to Alabama searching for gold. Eventually they left the area because their search was unsuccessful.

Although the Spanish didn't permanently settle in Alabama, their visits proved dangerous for Native Americans, many of whom were killed when the explorers took over their villages. Spanish explorers referred to the Cherokee, Creek, Choctaw, and Chickasaw as the Civilized Tribes because they adopted some European customs. Despite the fact that these Native Americans learned English and dressed in European-style clothing, they were usually not treated well by the explorers.

THE FRENCH SETTLE ALABAMA

After the Spanish left the area, French explorers arrived. French king Louis XIV sent Pierre Le Moyne d'Iberville and his brother, Jean Baptiste Le Moyne de Bienville, to establish a fort in the region. In 1702, the brothers founded Fort Louis de la Mobile on the Mobile River. Fort Louis became the capital of the region, which was known as the Louisiana Territory.

In 1711, a flood on the Mobile River destroyed Fort

Jean Baptiste (right) and Pierre Le Moyne (left) founded Fort Louis, the first permanent European settlement in Alabama.

Louis, and the French were forced to move south to present-day Mobile. There they established another settlement, also called Fort Louis, which became the first permanent European settlement in the Alabama area. It was renamed Fort Conde in 1720 and served as the capital of the Louisiana Territory until 1722.

SLAVERY IN ALABAMA

In the early 1700s, more settlers arrived from France and Canada. Farming became an important means of support for the colony. Colonists cleared the land to raise food to eat and sell. They produced sugar, rice, and indigo (a plant that produces blue dye), as well as tobacco.

To help clear the land, enslaved Africans were introduced into the colony in 1719. Captured in their homeland of Africa, men, women, and children were chained together and transported to North America on ships. Many Africans died on crowded slave ships. The ones who lived were sometimes separated from their families when they were auctioned off and sold to white landowners.

Enslaved Africans led difficult lives. They performed back-breaking labor on farms and were often treated harshly by their owners. They were usually not allowed to learn how to read and write. They didn't have the freedom to go where they pleased and were severely punished for trying to escape. Enslaved Africans gradually became an important source of labor for the growing colony.

France wasn't the only country with an interest in the New World. At the time, England and Spain claimed other parts of North America. They were all interested in the fur trade, which operated throughout most of the area. Animal furs could be sold for a profit in Europe, where they were used to make fashionable hats and muffs.

In the 1700s, a series of clashes erupted between Great Britain, France, and Spain as they fought for control of North America. In 1754, war broke out between France and Great Britain. Many Native Americans sided with the French because they feared that the British would take their land. The French and Indian War (1754–1763) ended in defeat for France. As a result, France was forced to turn over all the land east of the Mississippi River, including Alabama, to Great Britain.

In 1779, Spain declared war on Britain. A year later Spaniard Bernardo de Galvez captured Mobile, and the Mobile region was turned over to Spain. In 1783, northern Alabama became part of the United States. It wasn't until the War of 1812 (1812–1815) that Alabama was made whole again. During the war, the United States seized Mobile from Spain and officially claimed it as its own on

FAMOUS FIRSTS

- The Boll Weevil Monument in Enterprise is the first statue ever to honor an insect, 1919
- The Gaineswood Antebellum Home in Demopolis is the first house known to have running water, 1861
- The nation's first flight school was built in Montgomery by the Wright Brothers, 1910
- The first electric streetcar system was operated in Montgomery, 1886
- Isabella de Soto (wife of Spanish explorer Hernando de Soto) planted America's first fig trees at Fort Morgan

April 15, 1813. All of Alabama now belonged to the United States.

In 1817, the Alabama territory was organized as part of the United States. Saint Stephens served as its first capital.

FIGHTING FOR CONTROL

Although Alabama was now part of the United States, the fighting continued. Territorial arguments occurred between the Creeks and white settlers in Alabama. In the early 1800s, the Creeks lived mainly in two areas of Alabama—in central Alabama along the Coosa, Tuscaloosa, and Alabama Rivers, and in southeastern Alabama near the Chattahoochee River. Settlers arriving in Alabama often took land that belonged to the Creeks. In addition, they also expected the Creeks to adopt white ways. As a result, many Creeks became angry and frustrated.

At the same time, the United States and Britain continued to fight, as well. When the War of 1812 broke out between the two nations, some Creeks sided with Britain and fought against the United States army, while others joined forces with the United States against

During the War of 1812, many Native Americans joined the British in fighting against American soldiers.

Creek Chief Red Eagle surrendered to General Andrew Jackson after the Battle of Horseshoe Bend.

Britain. General Andrew Jackson won key victories against the Creek at the battles of Talladega and Horseshoe Bend.

When the war ended in 1815, many Creeks—as well as Cherokees, Choctaws, and Chickasaws—were forced to sign treaties, or agreements, that turned over much of their land in Alabama to the United States government. Although many Native Americans resisted leaving their homelands, Andrew Jackson forced their removal when he was elected president in 1828.

STATEHOOD AND THE CIVIL WAR

The days of Alabama being owned as a territory ended on December 14, 1819, when Alabama entered the Union as the 22nd state.

This drawing shows a view of the capitol in Montgomery in 1857.

Huntsville served as the capital until 1820, when the state capital was moved to Cahaba. Six years later, the capital was moved again, this time to Tuscaloosa. In 1846, the state legislature voted to move the state capital to Montgomery, its fourth and final destination. By 1851, the present capitol building was complete.

During the 1800s, Alabama grew quickly. Settlers continued to arrive in Alabama, and life revolved around large farms called plantations. Cotton was one of Alabama's most important crops.

Mobile, the state's only seaport, became the nation's second-largest cotton exporter by 1860. The plantation way of life required a large workforce, and enslaved Africans were brought in at a steady pace to keep production going. In 1860 there were more than 430,000 slaves in Alabama and a free population of fewer than 520,000.

Slave labor was considered essential not only in Alabama, but in other southern states, as well, including Virginia, North Carolina, South Carolina, Mississippi, and Georgia. Many Northerners, however, felt that slavery was wrong. It was illegal in most northern states and also in some new states that joined the Union during the 1800s.

Alabama's cotton industry—including the picking, bailing, and ginning of cotton—depended on slave labor.

When Abraham Lincoln was elected president in 1860, the South feared that he would abolish slavery. To protect their right to own slaves, some southern states seceded from the Union. On January 11, 1861, after forty-two years of statehood, Alabama left the Union and joined a newly created nation called the Confederate States of America. Jefferson Davis was elected its first president. Montgomery served as the first capital of the Confederacy, and as a result, Alabama became known as the Cradle of the Confederacy.

Tension between North and South grew, and in 1861 the Civil War (1861–1865) broke out. Most Alabamians fought on the Confederate side, but some 2,500 white Alabamians and 10,000 African Americans fought for the North (the Union). In August 1864, the Union

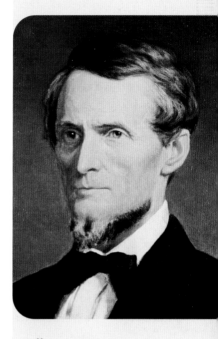

Jefferson Davis was inaugurated President of the Confederate States at the capitol in Montgomery.

Union Admiral David Farragut led an attack on Confederate forces at Mobile Bay.

29

WHAT'S IN A NAME?

Many names and places in Alabama have interesting origins.

Name	Comes From or Means
Alabama	From Choctaw words meaning "thicket clearers" or "vegetation gatherers;" referring to the Alabama Indians
Blount County	Tennessee governor Willie G. Blount
Decatur	Stephen Decatur, an Alabama naval hero
Dothan	A biblical verse, Genesis 37:17, which reads, "For I heard them say, let us go to Dothan."
Huntsville	John Hunt, founder of Huntsville
Montgomery	Richard Montgomery, a Revolutionary War general
Selma	From a Gaelic poem, means "high seat" or "throne"
Tuscaloosa	Native American Chief Tuskaloosa

won an important naval battle in Mobile Bay, effectively closing off a major supply channel for the Confederates.

The last major battle of the Civil War took place at Fort Blakeley in Alabama. On April 9, 1865—six hours after General Robert E. Lee surrendered his Confederate troops in Virginia—Union troops defeated Confederate soldiers in the Battle of Blakeley. The North had won the Civil War.

RECONSTRUCTION

After the Civil War, Alabama's economy was in ruins. The plantation system broke down without slavery, and many Alabamians became sharecroppers. Landowners rented out land to sharecroppers and provided them with tools, money, seeds, and shelter. In return, the sharecropper paid the owner of the land with the crops they harvested. This system worked in favor of the landowners and kept many sharecroppers from ever making a profit.

As a result of the war, Alabama's almost 500,000 African Americans were freed. Freedmen suddenly found themselves poverty-stricken, without work and a way to support themselves. In March 1865, the Freedman's Bureau was established to help former slaves find jobs and places to live.

In 1868, Alabama adopted a new constitution, or plan of government. The constitution protected the rights of African Americans, who were now citizens of the United States. With the ratification of the new constitution, Alabama was readmitted to the United States on June 25, 1868.

Despite their status as citizens, African Americans were treated poorly by whites. Whites all over the South, including those in Alabama, resisted the changes taking place. They tried to hold back progress for African Americans. Some southerners formed groups such as the Ku Klux Klan

Members of the Ku Klux Klan terrorized and killed African Americans under cover of night.

(KKK) to terrorize and kill African Americans. Similar organizations, such as the White Brotherhood and the Men of Peace, operated mainly in southern Alabama. In 1901, Alabama's constitution was rewritten, taking away the right of African Americans—and poor white immigrants—to vote.

THE GROWTH OF INDUSTRY

In the early 1900s, an insect called the boll weevil shook the foundations of Alabama's farming industry. Boll weevils fed on the boll, or blossom, of cotton plants, and they eventually destroyed cotton harvests across Alabama. As a result, farmers began growing other crops, such as peanuts. Although the boll weevil plague was devastating at the time, it forced many Alabamians to find other ways to make a living.

The construction of railroads helped other industries to develop. In 1871, the city of Birmingham was founded at the intersection of two railroad lines. Coal, iron ore, and limestone were abundant around Birmingham, and it quickly became one of the South's most important industrial centers. Iron and steel mills were started throughout the area. Other industries, such as shipping, lumbering, and textile manufacturing, also developed throughout Alabama.

Birmingham was home to many furnaces like this one, where workers produced pig iron for use in mills and factories.

Alabama's role as an industrial center helped to strengthen its economy during World War I (1914–1918). Mobile became an important shipbuilding center, and Alabama's steel factories supplied materials for the war against Germany and Austria-Hungary. About 74,000 Alabamians fought in the war, and more than 6,000 died.

THE GREAT DEPRESSION AND WORLD WAR II

The economic boom of the early 1900s didn't last long. When the stock market crashed in 1929, people all over the United States, including Alabama, lost huge amounts of money. They could no longer afford to buy things, and businesses suffered as a result. Many companies shut down, leaving thousands of people without jobs. Hard times fell on the country, as people struggled just to buy food and pay for their homes. This period is known as the Great Depression (1929–1939).

In 1933, President Franklin D. Roosevelt helped create the Tennessee Valley Authority (TVA). This government agency was formed to plan for the use and conservation of the Tennessee River basin. The TVA built dams, replanted forests, and taught farmers how to produce better crops. Alabamians benefited from many of the TVA's projects, including several hydroelectric facilities that were built together with river dams. Powered by water, these facilities produced electricity. Electric lights and modern appliances made life easier and farms more productive.

The start of World War II (1939–1945) helped bring an end to the Great Depression. Once again, Alabama products and services were needed for wartime production. Alabama became an important center for shipbuilding and rocket production. Mobile shipyards built warships, and Talladega powder plants produced explosives for use on the ships. Defense plants and military bases were built in Alabama because land was cheap and the climate was pleasant. Many Alabama towns flourished as a result of these industries, including Mobile, Huntsville, and Childersburg.

About 320,000 Alabamians served in World War II, and more than 4,000 lost their lives. The Tuskegee airmen were among the Alabama residents that served in World War II. This unit of African-American fighter pilots trained at Tuskegee Institute.

African Americans trained at Tuskegee Air Field made a major contribution to the war effort.

In the 1950s and 1960s, African Americans in the South continued to lose ground when it came to their civil rights. They couldn't stay in most hotels or eat in certain restaurants. They were forced to use separate facilities, such as waiting rooms, water fountains, and entrances labeled "Colored," a term that indicated the difference in skin color between whites and African Americans. This type of separation between African Americans and whites was known as segregation. In Alabama, as in other southern states, it was not against the law to discriminate against African Americans.

In the 1950s and 1960s, many people fought against such discrimination. Civil-rights activists led protests and demonstrations in an effort to change the laws. However, civil-rights demonstrations were sometimes dangerous. Some people were beaten and arrested, while others were controlled by snarling police dogs and tear-gas.

Alabama, in particular, became a center for civil-rights struggles. Many important events in the history of the civil-rights movement took place in Alabama. On December 1, 1955, in Montgomery, an African-American woman named Rosa Parks refused to give up her seat on the city bus to a white passenger. Her actions were against the law in Alabama, and Rosa Parks was arrested. Her arrest prompted civil-rights leaders to stage a bus boycott. African Americans refused to ride Montgomery city

EXTRA! EXTRA!

Rosa Parks is sometimes called the Mother of the Civil Rights Movement. Her actions started a chain of events that ultimately led to the end of segregation in the South. She was inducted into the National Women's Hall of Fame in 1993. Rosa Parks died in 2005 at the age of 92.

buses for more than a year. In November 1956, the United States Supreme Court declared that segregation, or separation, on city buses was unconstitutional.

Tension between African Americans and whites continued to build. A series of bombings occurred in Birmingham, and on September 15, 1963, a bomb at the 16th Street Baptist Church killed four young girls. The tragedy had a dramatic effect on the civil-rights movement, prompting more people to speak out against segregation in Alabama. In 1964, President Lyndon B. Johnson signed the Civil Rights Act, which protected the rights of African-American citizens and put an end to segregation in restaurants, movie theaters, and other public places.

Rosa Parks's refusal to give up her bus seat sparked the beginning of the civil-rights movement.

However, African Americans and whites were still far from equal. Another major demonstration took place in 1965, when civil-rights leader Dr. Martin Luther King Jr. led more than 500 people on a 54-mile (87-km) march from Selma to Montgomery. In response, President Johnson signed the Voting Rights Act of 1965, guaranteeing African Americans the right to vote.

There was still much progress to be made. Although segregated schools were illegal, Alabama governor George Wallace traveled to the University of Alabama and several public schools to personally prevent African Americans from entering. The Alabama National Guard was called in to force the governor to step aside and allow African-American students to enter the school safely and peacefully. By the early 1970s, nearly 8 of every 10 African-American students attended integrated schools.

On November 6, 1963, Governor George Wallace blocked a doorway at the University of Alabama in order to prevent African-American students from entering.

MAKING PROGRESS

Segregation did not really end in Alabama until the 1980s. Throughout the 1960s and 1970s, however, African Americans played key roles in local and state politics. In 1966, Lucius Amerson was elected sheriff of Macon County. He was the first African American in the South to be elected to such an office. In 1979, an African-American politician named Richard Arrington was elected mayor of Birmingham. Just sixteen years earlier, Birmingham's police department had used attack dogs on civil-rights marchers.

The Tennessee-Tombigbee waterway travels through southern Alabama to the Gulf of Mexico.

Even Governor George Wallace changed with the times. During his governorship in the 1970s, Wallace appointed several African Americans to state offices.

MODERN ALABAMA

In the 1980s and 1990s, Alabama experienced economic changes. In 1985, the completion of the Tennessee-Tombigbee Waterway allowed the state to link the port of Mobile with ports along the Tennessee and Ohio rivers. As a result, the importance of Mobile as a port began steadily increasing. Ships regularly deliver minerals and other raw materials to Mobile Bay for use in Alabama's factories. Other ships export Alabama products such as coal, iron, steel, petroleum, wood, soybeans, and wheat to sell in other states and countries.

The government also began looking for ways to expand Alabama's manufacturing industries. In 1997, Mercedes-Benz built an automobile assembly plant in Alabama.

By the 1990s, manufacturing was one of the most important industries in the state.

Today, Alabama is a vital part of America's future as well as its history. Not only is Alabama important to our nation's growth and economy, it is also a great place to live, work, and visit.

EXTRA! EXTRA!

In the 1990s, there was disagreement among Alabamians about an important symbol of the state's past—the Confederacy. For many years the Alabama state flag featured the symbol of the Confederacy, and the Confederate battle flag itself flew over the state capitol. Some people consider the symbol to be one of slavery and racism, while others think it represents an important part of their history that should not be forgotten. In 1993, the Alabama government decided to remove all symbols of the Confederacy from the capitol. Some groups still protest the decision.

CHAPTER FOUR

GOVERNING ALABAMA

Alabama's capitol has been the scene of some important historical events, such as the Civil Rights March and the swearing in of Jefferson Davis, president of the Confederacy.

Because the people's views of government have changed throughout history, the state's constitution has also changed. A constitution explains how the government will run the state and protect the rights of its people. Alabama has had six constitutions: in 1819, 1861, 1865, 1868, 1875, and 1901. Today, Alabama still uses the 1901 constitution.

Lawmakers can amend, or change, the constitution at any time, as long as the change has been approved by a majority of voters. The Alabama constitution has been amended more than 650 times, making it one of the longest of any state.

Alabama's state government is organized in the same way as the United States government. It is divided into three branches, or parts: the legislative, the executive, and the judicial.

EXECUTIVE BRANCH

The executive branch enforces and carries out the laws. The governor is head of the executive branch. He or she is elected by the people of Alabama. To become governor, a person must be a resident of Alabama for at least seven years and a United States citizen for at least ten years. The governor of Alabama is elected to a four-year term and cannot serve more than two terms in a row.

The governor promises to uphold Alabama's laws. He or she decides how the state's money will be spent, whether on education or the building of roads and parks. The governor also has the power to assemble the state's army, called the Alabama National Guard, in case of emergency. New laws that are proposed by the legislature (Alabama's lawmaking body) may be vetoed (turned down) by the governor. However, a majority of legislators may vote to override, or disregard, his or her decision. The lieutenant governor works closely with the governor to make sure the state runs smoothly.

Other members of the executive branch include the attorney general, the secretary of state, the state treasurer, and the state auditor. These elected officials each serve a four-year term and may serve consecutive, or repeated, terms.

The attorney general serves as the legal representative of the state. His or her job is to enforce state laws and protect the state's legal interests. If someone brings a lawsuit against Alabama, the attorney general would represent the state's side of the case.

Alabama's secretary of state has more than a thousand duties that involve processing and filing important documents. The secretary of state is in charge of caring for and preserving documents in four categories: executive, legislative, elections, and business. These records include the official seal of the state of Alabama, the names of registered voters, and information about Alabama's businesses.

The state treasurer and the state auditor manage the money belonging to the state, including money from taxes paid by citizens and funds provided by the United States government. This money is used to sup-

The Secretary of State's suite, shown here, is located in the state capitol.

port Alabama's public schools and universities. It is also used to maintain roads, streets, and parks, and to pay the salaries of government workers such as police officers.

LEGISLATIVE BRANCH

Alabama's legislature is divided into two sections—the house of representatives and the senate. There are 105 members in the house of representatives and 35 state senators, each of whom is elected to serve a four-year term. The Alabama legislature meets for thirty days each year.

The legislative branch makes state laws. For example, in 1999 lawmakers approved a law requiring all Alabama drivers to purchase automobile insurance. The legislature also recently approved the hiring of 200 additional teachers for public schools. In addition, the legislature decides how much money will be used to operate state agencies such as the bureau of motor vehicles and the parks department.

JUDICIAL BRANCH

The judicial branch determines the meaning of laws. The Alabama court system is responsible for deciding whether a law has been broken. The judicial branch is made up of the supreme court, the court of civil appeals, the court of criminal appeals, circuit courts, district courts, probate courts, and municipal courts.

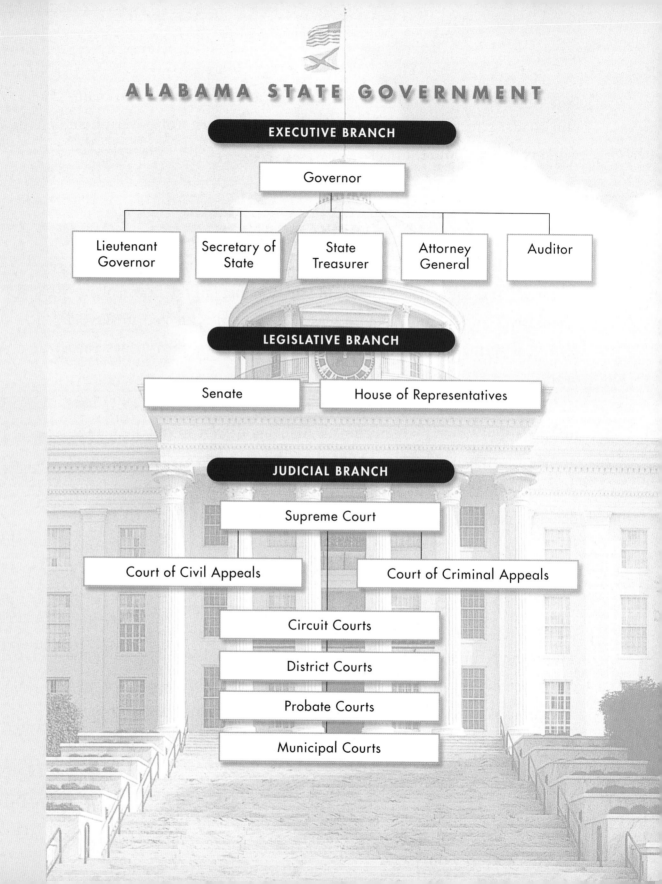

ALABAMA STATE GOVERNMENT

EXECUTIVE BRANCH

Governor

- Lieutenant Governor
- Secretary of State
- State Treasurer
- Attorney General
- Auditor

LEGISLATIVE BRANCH

Senate

House of Representatives

JUDICIAL BRANCH

Supreme Court

Court of Civil Appeals

Court of Criminal Appeals

Circuit Courts

District Courts

Probate Courts

Municipal Courts

ALABAMA GOVERNORS

Name	Term	Name	Term
William W. Bibb	1819–1820	Joseph F. Johnston	1896–1900
Thomas Bibb	1820–1821	William D. Jelks	1900 (Dec.)
Israel Pickens	1821–1825	William J. Samford	1900–1901
John Murphy	1825–1829	William D. Jelks	1901–1907
Gabriel Moore	1829–1831	Russell Cunningham	1904–1905
Samuel B. Moore	1831	Braxton B. Comer	1907–1911
John Gayle	1831–1835	Emmett O'Neal	1911–1915
Clement C. Clay	1835–1837	Charles Henderson	1915–1919
Hugh McVay	1837	Thomas E. Kilby	1919–1923
Arthur P. Bagby	1837–1841	William W. Brandon	1923–1927
Benjamin Fitzpatrick	1841–1845	Bibb Graves	1927–1931
Joshua L. Martin	1845–1847	Benjamin M. Miller	1931–1935
Reuben Chapman	1847–1849	Bibb Graves	1935–1939
Henry W. Collier	1849–1853	Frank M. Dixon	1939–1943
John A. Winston	1853–1857	Chauncey M. Sparks	1943–1947
Andrew B. Moore	1857–1861	James E. Folsom	1947–1951
John G. Shorter	1861–1863	Gordon Persons	1951–1955
Thomas H. Watts	1863–1865	James E. Folsom	1955–1959
Lewis E. Parsons	1865	John M. Patterson	1959–1963
Robert M. Patton	1865–1867	George C. Wallace	1963–1967
Wager Swayne	1867–1868	Lurleen B. Wallace	1967–1968
William H. Smith	1868–1870	Albert P. Brewer	1968–1971
Robert B. Lindsay	1870–1872	George C. Wallace	1971–1979
David P. Lewis	1872–1874	Forrest James	1979–1983
George S. Houston	1874–1878	George C. Wallace	1983–1987
Rufus W. Cobb	1878–1882	Guy Hunt	1987–1993
Edward A. O'Neal	1882–1886	James E. Folsom Jr.	1993–1995
Thomas Seay	1886–1890	Forrest "Fob" James	1995–1999
Thomas G. Jones	1890–1894	Don Siegelman	1999–2003
William C. Oates	1894–1896	Bob Riley	2003–

The supreme court is the highest court in the state. The Alabama supreme court hears appeals, or cases that have already been heard in a lower court, to determine the fairness of the decision. A chief justice (judge) and eight associate judges oversee this court. They are elected to six-year terms.

Below the supreme court are the court of criminal appeals and the court of civil appeals. Five judges serve on each court; they are also elected to six-year terms. These judges appeal, or challenge, decisions made by the circuit courts.

Circuit courts hear both criminal and civil trials. A criminal trail would involve a person charged with a crime, and a civil trial usually involves money or property issues. Lower courts are the district, probate, and municipal courts.

This is a view of the intersection of Tallapoosa and Commerce Streets in Montgomery.

TAKE A TOUR OF MONTGOMERY, THE STATE CAPITAL

Alabama is a blend of the old and new South. Nowhere is this more obvious than in its capital city, Montgomery. Located near the middle of the state along the Alabama River, Montgomery is an attractive mix of modern skyscrapers and historic buildings. More than 200,000 people live in Montgomery.

The city is steeped in history. It was named for Revolutionary War hero General Richard Montgomery. Montgomery is famous as the first city in the country to have electric streetcars and the first place to have a flight school. It is also known as the city where Rosa Parks, Dr. Martin Luther King Jr., and hundreds of other Americans marched for civil rights.

The capitol building sits above downtown Montgomery on what is known as Goat Hill. The hill, originally owned by Montgomery's founder, Andrew Dexter, got its name from the goats that once grazed there. Dexter gave the land to the city to build the capitol, and the original structure was completed in 1847. Two years later the capitol was destroyed by fire, and it was reconstructed in 1851.

The design of the building is called Greek revival, patterned after buildings in Greece. It is made of white Alabama marble and has a dome with a stained-glass skylight. On the building's steps is a bronze star, signifying the spot where Jefferson Davis stood when he became president of the Confederate

Murals inside the capitol dome depict scenes from Alabama's history.

EXTRA! EXTRA!

Before the first official governor's residence was established in 1911, Alabama governors lived in private homes or local hotels. Since then, the state has had three official governor's residences. The first, a brownstone, was purchased in 1911. The second was the former home of an Alabama general. The third and current governor's mansion also belonged to a former general. Built in 1907, it is white with columns in the front (shown right). In the mid-1970s, a pool in the shape of Alabama was constructed in the backyard.

States of America. Inside the capitol, murals illustrate the history of Alabama in colorful pictures.

Across the street from the capitol is the first White House of the Confederacy, where Jefferson Davis lived after he was elected president of the Confederacy. Three months later, Davis and his family moved to the new Confederate capital in Richmond, Virginia. You can learn more about him by touring the house and viewing his personal items, photographs, and documents on display.

A block from the capitol is the Dexter Avenue King Memorial Baptist Church, where Martin Luther King Jr. began his career as a minister. Today, it is one of the most historic places in Montgomery. Visitors can

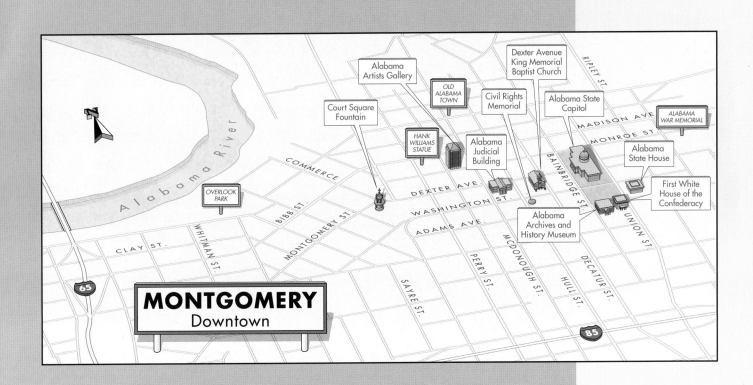

Alabama Artists Gallery

Dexter Avenue King Memorial Baptist Church

OLD ALABAMA TOWN

Civil Rights Memorial

Alabama State Capitol

ALABAMA WAR MEMORIAL

Court Square Fountain

HANK WILLIAMS STATUE

Alabama Judicial Building

Alabama State House

First White House of the Confederacy

Alabama River

COMMERCE

OVERLOOK PARK

BIBB ST.

DEXTER AVE.

WASHINGTON ST.

MADISON AVE.

MONROE ST.

BAINBRIDGE ST.

RIPLEY ST.

Alabama Archives and History Museum

ADAMS AVE.

UNION ST.

CLAY ST.

WHITMAN ST.

MONTGOMERY ST.

SAYRE ST.

PERRY ST.

McDONOUGH ST.

HULL ST.

DECATUR ST.

MONTGOMERY
Downtown

65

85

tour the basement of the church and see a film that explains Dr. King's work during the civil-rights movement. A wall mural highlights King's role as one of America's most important civil-rights leaders.

Within walking distance of the capitol is the Civil Rights Memorial. The memorial is dedicated to the forty people who died between 1954 and 1968 because of their involvement in the civil-rights movement. Maya Lin, designer of the Vietnam Veterans Memorial in Washington, D.C., designed the memorial, a circular black granite table and a black granite wall covered with flowing water. The name and story of each civil-rights supporter is etched on the memorial, along

Every year, Montgomery's Civil Rights Memorial inspires thousands of visitors from around the world.

with the following quote by Dr. Martin Luther King Jr.: "We are not satisfied and we will not be satisfied until justice rolls down like water, and righteousness like a mighty stream."

Another interesting historical site in Montgomery is Old Alabama Town. This historic site includes 35 restored buildings, including slave quarters, pioneer cabins, a one-room schoolhouse, a drugstore museum, and a working cotton gin, that offer a look at how Alabamians lived in the 1800s.

FIND OUT MORE

Maya Lin said her design of the Civil Rights Memorial is "not a monument to suffering; it is a memorial to hope." If you could design a memorial to the civil-rights movement in America, what would it look like?

CHAPTER FIVE

THE PEOPLE AND PLACES OF ALABAMA

The Birmingham skyline sparkles at dusk.

There are about 4,599,030 people living in Alabama today. The state ranks 23rd among the states in population.

Of these residents, 7 of every 10 are of European descent. One of every 4 Alabamians is African-American and almost 2 of every 100 people are Hispanic. Slightly more than 1 of every 100 people are Native American or Asian.

Alabamians have diverse backgrounds. Many are related to early settlers who came to Alabama from Ireland, France, England, Scotland, Germany, and Canada. People who now settle in the state also come from countries such as Taiwan, Mexico, Laos, Vietnam, India, and China.

MUSIC AND SPORTS FAME

Alabamians have made many important contributions to our nation's history, particularly in music and sports. Alabama is part of the South, the

54

region of the United States that gave birth to almost all types of "American" music, including blues, country, bluegrass, jazz, and rock 'n' roll. These types of music evolved from and were influenced by various cultural groups in the South such as Native Americans, African Americans, and Europeans, such as the Irish and French settlers.

William Christopher "W.C." Handy was an African-American musician born in Florence in 1873. He was called the "Father of the Blues." As a child, W.C. heard the songs of African-American farm workers. Their sad, hopeful songs inspired him to create a type of jazz called blues. The blues became popular in the early 1900s. One of his most famous songs is "St. Louis Blues." His childhood home is now a museum where visitors can see his piano, trumpet, and handwritten music sheets.

Hiram "Hank" Williams taught himself to play the guitar as a child.

Many people would agree that one of the greatest country singers of all time came from Alabama. Hank Williams Sr. was born in Georgianna in 1923. A singer and a songwriter, he was known as the "King of Country Music." In downtown Montgomery, there is a life-size statue of Williams holding a guitar. Today, his son, Hank Williams Jr., is also a popular singer. R&B star Lionel Ritchie and country music band Alabama are also from the state.

Alabama has produced many sports legends, from baseball players to Olympic athletes to coaches. Leroy "Satchel" Paige was a legendary baseball pitcher born in Mobile. He was elected to the Baseball Hall of Fame in 1971. An African-American runner from Oakville became one of the most famous Olympic athletes in history. Jesse Owens won four gold medals at the 1936 Olympics in Berlin. And Paul "Bear" Bryant, an Arkansas native who played football for the University of Alabama, is considered one of the greatest college football coaches in history. During his 38-year career as head football coach at the University of Alabama, his team won 323 victories.

WHO'S WHO IN ALABAMA?

Henry "Hank" Aaron (1934–), known as "Hammerin' Hank," was born in Mobile in 1934. This talented baseball player set the all-time home-run record with 755 home runs. This record lasted until 2007, when it was broken by Barry Bonds. Aaron was named to the Baseball Hall of Fame in 1982.

Jesse Owens was one of the greatest track and field stars of the early 20th century.

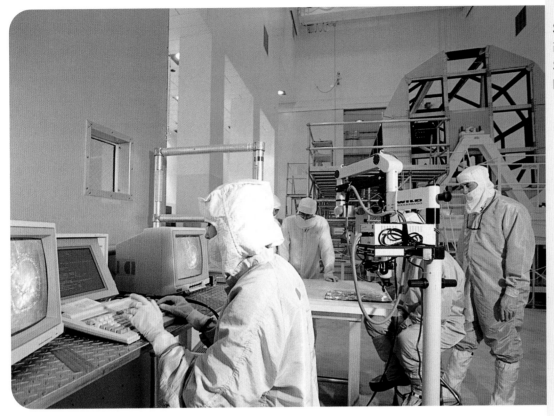

Scientists do space research in a laboratory at Marshall Space Flight Center in Huntsville.

WORKING IN ALABAMA

Most Alabamians work in service industries. These positions include teachers, store clerks, food servers, police officers, postal workers, and bus drivers. Finance, insurance, healthcare, and real estate are growing service areas in Alabama. Birmingham is the state's leading financial center and the headquarters for two major banking companies in the South. Government jobs are also part of Alabama's service industry. Maxwell Air Force Base and Gunter Annex, near Montgomery, and the George C. Marshall Space Flight Center and Redstone Arsenal in the Huntsville area all employ government workers.

Part of the service industry includes tourism, the business of providing food, shelter, and entertainment for visitors. Tourism is big business in Alabama—more than 18 million tourists visited the state in 2002. The Gulf Coast is a popular place for tourists to fish, swim, and enjoy other water sports. During late March and early April, Alabama is ablaze with beautiful azalea blossoms along Mobile's "Azalea Trail." The May festival in Mobile features colorful parades during the day and at night. Visitors also come to Alabama to tour its many historic homes and gardens. About 137,000 Alabamians work in the tourist industry.

Manufacturing is one of Alabama's most important industries. Many residents work in factories to produce chemicals, textiles (such as fabric, yarn, and thread), clothing, electronic equipment, and rubber and plastic products. Paper products, such as pulp, paper bags, and tissue, are

Alabama is known for its steel-making industry, which is concentrated in the northern part of the state.

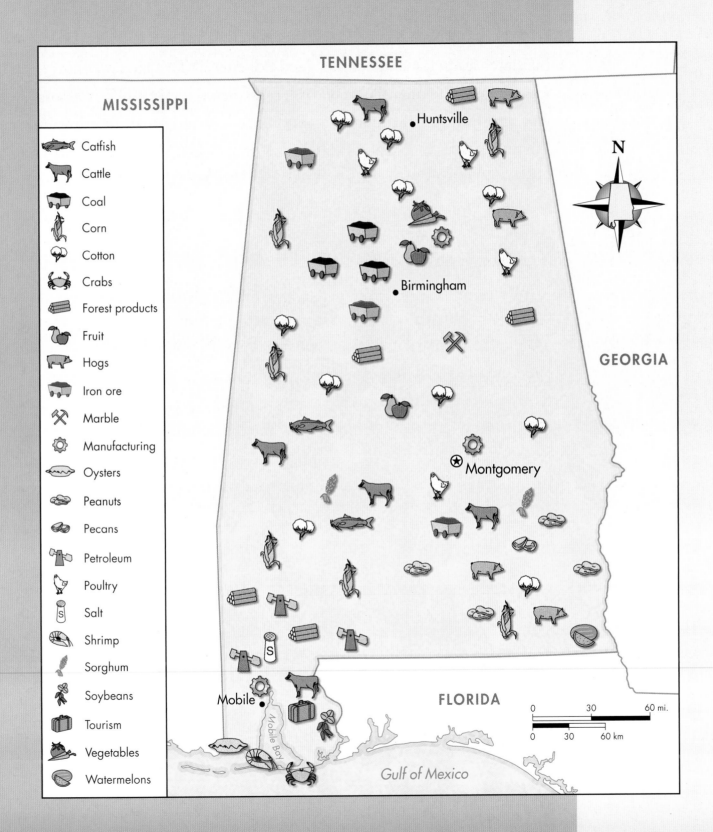

TENNESSEE

MISSISSIPPI

GEORGIA

FLORIDA

Gulf of Mexico

Mobile Bay

• Huntsville

• Birmingham

⭐ Montgomery

Mobile •

Legend

- Catfish
- Cattle
- Coal
- Corn
- Cotton
- Crabs
- Forest products
- Fruit
- Hogs
- Iron ore
- Marble
- Manufacturing
- Oysters
- Peanuts
- Pecans
- Petroleum
- Poultry
- Salt
- Shrimp
- Sorghum
- Soybeans
- Tourism
- Vegetables
- Watermelons

N

0   30   60 mi.

0   30   60 km

the state's leading manufactured goods. Siemens VDO has an electronics company in Huntsville, and a Mercedes-Benz factory is in Tuscaloosa County. Fruit of the Loom makes athletic and casual clothing in Alexander City. Steelmaking is an important activity in Birmingham, Decatur, and Gadsden. Many companies choose to locate in Alabama because of the state's good quality of life, excellent workforce, and low cost of doing business.

Although farming is not as important as it was in the past, it still contributes much money to the state. Broilers (young chickens) and beef cattle are the leading farm products. Farmers in Alabama also grow cotton, soybeans, pecans, potatoes, sweet potatoes, sweet corn, and tomatoes. There are about 43,000 farms in Alabama. Today's farms are decreasing in number. Fewer Alabamians work in farming now because modern machinery has taken over much of the work.

Some Alabamians work in the fishing industry. Crabs, oysters, shrimp, mussels, and fish, including mullet and snapper, are caught mainly in the Gulf of Mexico.

TAKE A TOUR OF ALABAMA

Mobile

The perfect place to start our tour of Alabama is in Mobile, the state's oldest and second-largest city. Located on the Gulf of Mexico, Mobile is

Pecans are one of Alabama's most important crops. In fact, it is the official state nut. Every year, Alabama ranks from fifth to seventh in the country for pecan production. This recipe for caramel pecan turtles makes a tasty Alabama treat.

CARAMEL PECAN TURTLES

145 small pecan halves (about 1 cup)
36 vanilla caramels
1/2 cup semisweet chocolate chips

1. Preheat oven to 325°.
2. Grease a cookie sheet with cooking oil.
3. On the cookie sheet, arrange 5 pecans together to create a turtle's legs and head. Place one caramel in the center of the pecan turtle.
4. Repeat step 3 until you've used all the pecans and caramels.
5. Bake in the oven just a few minutes, or until caramels are soft.
6. Remove the cookie sheet from oven and flatten caramel centers with a spatula.
7. Put chocolate chips in a small pan. Melt chips on a low setting on the stove.
8. Spoon melted chocolate chips over caramel centers.
9. Let your Alabama turtles cool before serving.

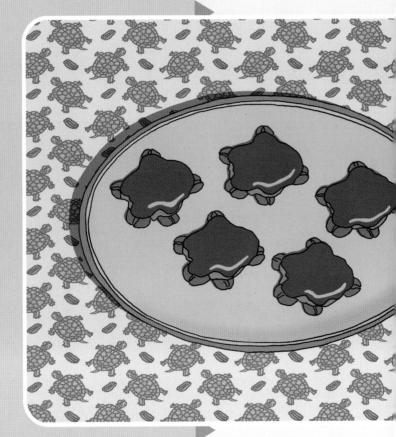

home to the Port of Alabama, one of the busiest ports in the country. Every year, millions of tons of products are shipped from this port to places around the world.

One of the highlights of the city's waterfront is a World War II battleship called the USS *Alabama*. The crew of the USS *Alabama* shot down twenty-two enemy planes during World War II. After the war, the ship was docked in Seattle, where it was to be sold and turned into scrap metal. To save the battleship, Alabamians raised enough money to move

The USS *Alabama* was used during World War II.

it to Mobile Bay, where it stands today. Visitors can tour the battleship to learn more about its history.

Other interesting sites in Mobile include the Museum of Mobile, where you'll find exhibits that cover more than 300 years of Mobile history. Bellingrath Gardens and Home is an internationally known public garden that is open for tours. After spending some time in the garden, take a leisurely river cruise down the Isle Aux Oies River.

Northeast of Mobile is Montgomery, Alabama's capital city. Be sure to visit the capitol building and Dexter Avenue Baptist Church. After that, stop by the Alabama Department of Archives & History. Housed in a marble building, the archives include many exhibits about Alabama's history, including Native Americans and the state's military. There's also a hands-on gallery for children called Grandma's Attic.

From Montgomery, travel about an hour east to get to the next stop on our tour, Tuskegee. At Tuskegee Institute National Historic Site you'll learn about inventor George Washington Carver at the George Washington Carver Museum. The museum is dedicated to the man who invented, among many things, peanut butter. Carver also discovered 118 uses for sweet potatoes, including using it to make candy, medicine, and shoe polish. On the same grounds you will find The Oaks, home of Booker T. Washington. Washington was a famous African-American educator and the respected leader of Tuskegee Institute.

To the west of Montgomery is Selma, where the past comes to life. Selma has the largest historic

George Washington Carver is one of our nation's best-known scientists.

FIND OUT MORE

At Tuskegee Institute, George Washington Carver discovered more than 300 products that could be made from peanuts. His inventions using peanuts included peanut butter, candy, coffee, face cream, gasoline, ink, insecticide, and soap. What other products can you think of that contain peanuts?

district in the state. To better understand the civil-rights movement, take the Martin Luther King Jr. Street Historic Walking Tour. This self-guided tour is made up of 20 memorials highlighting the history of the fight for voting rights in Selma. The First Baptist Church, George Washington Carver's home, and the Martin Luther King Jr. monument are just a few of the historic treasures on this tour.

Our next stop is Birmingham, in the center of the state. The Alabama Jazz Hall of Fame is a good place to learn about the development of jazz and about famous jazz musicians with ties to Alabama, such as Lionel Hampton and Erskin Hawkins. At the Alabama Sports Hall of Fame, you'll find trophies and awards that belonged to Alabama sports legends, including coach Paul "Bear" Bryant, boxer Joe Louis, and Olympic athlete Jesse Owens. The uniforms, equipment, and photographs of these sports heroes are on display.

The Sloss Furnaces National Historic Landmark in Birmingham is the only museum of its kind in the world. The museum features a furnace plant where iron was made for nearly a hundred

This exhibit at the Alabama Sports Hall of Fame depicts Joe Louis, a famous boxer from Alabama.

65

Camels are at home in the Birmingham zoo.

years. It is now a center for the creation and display of metal art.

Another fun place to visit is the Birmingham Zoo. The zoo is home to more than 1,000 animals from around the world, including some that are endangered, such as the Aruba Island rattlesnake and the Puerto Rican Crested toad. You can see the animals from a seat on the zoo train, or walk through the zoo and explore the tropical rain forest and the Alligator Bayou. You can also watch sea lions being trained and fed at the zoo.

Tuscaloosa, west of Birmingham, is home to the University of Alabama. There are several museums on campus, including one dedicated to the college's most famous football coach, the Paul W. Bryant Museum. At the museum you'll find jerseys, photographs, and trophies of the Crimson Tide players, as well as videos that highlight important moments of the team.

Other museums worth visiting include the Children's Hands-On Museum in Tuscaloosa, which has interactive exhibits about art, history, and the environment. Among the exhibits are a Choctaw village and a planetarium. At the Alabama Museum of Natural History, rocks, minerals, and fossils from the dinosaur and ice ages are on display. Also on exhibit is the only meteorite known to have struck a human.

Just a short drive from Tuscaloosa is Moundville, the site of more than 25 prehistoric mounds. You can tour the museum's Native American village and nature trails on the banks of the Black Warrior River. Moundville is also the site of the Moundville Native American festival. Every year, performers and artisans of Cherokee, Chickasaw, Seminole, Creek, and Choctaw descent gather at Moundville to celebrate their rich heritage. Among other things, the festival features flintknappers reproducing traditional stone tools and arrowheads, and a living history camp from the year 1800 that includes costumed actors.

These Choctaw dancers are participating in the Moundville Native American festival.

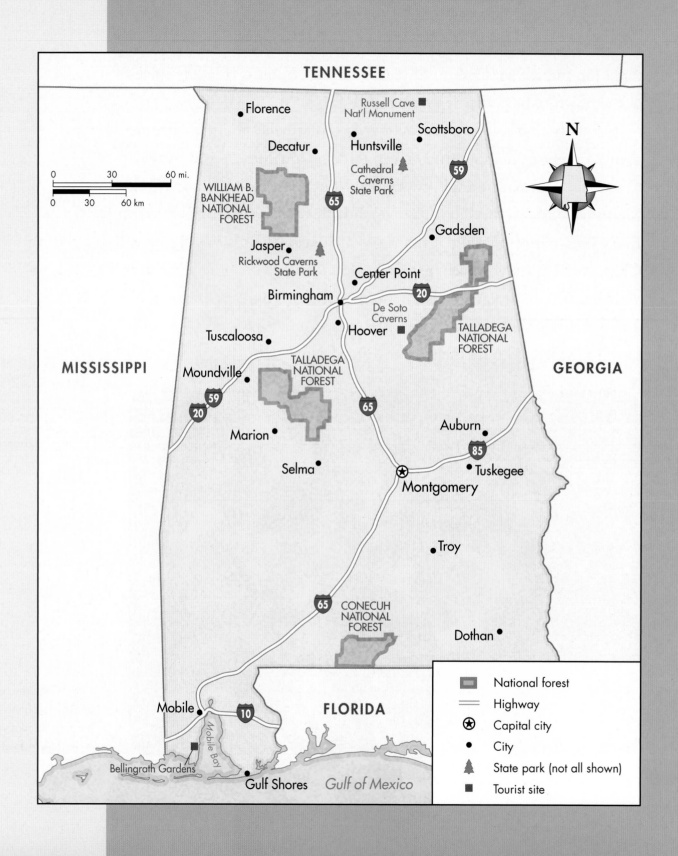

TENNESSEE

Florence

Russell Cave
Nat'l Monument

Scottsboro

Decatur

Huntsville

Cathedral
Caverns
State Park

59

WILLIAM B.
BANKHEAD
NATIONAL
FOREST

65

Gadsden

Jasper

Rickwood Caverns
State Park

Center Point

Birmingham

De Soto
Caverns

20

TALLADEGA
NATIONAL
FOREST

Hoover

Tuscaloosa

MISSISSIPPI

Moundville

59

20

TALLADEGA
NATIONAL
FOREST

GEORGIA

Marion

65

Auburn

85

Selma

Tuskegee

Montgomery

Troy

Dothan

65

CONECUH
NATIONAL
FOREST

Mobile

10

FLORIDA

Bellingrath Gardens

Mobile Bay

Gulf Shores

Gulf of Mexico

	National forest
	Highway
⊛	Capital city
•	City
🌲	State park (not all shown)
■	Tourist site

On the drive north, stop at Guntersville Lake, the largest lake in Alabama. It is popular for activities such as swimming, fishing, and water skiing.

In northern Alabama, Huntsville is the home of the U.S. Space and Rocket Center, the largest space museum in the world. Nicknamed Rocket City, U.S.A., Huntsville greets thousands of visitors every year. The museum offers demonstrations and hands-on exhibits about the past, present, and future of space exploration. Visitors can take a NASA bus tour, see the center's employees build rocket parts, and take a "ride" to Mars. The center is also the site of a space camp where kids can become junior astronauts.

There's so much to see and do in Alabama. Whether you're interested in learning about history or exploring the future, there's something for everyone in Alabama.

The U.S. Space and Rocket Center features a full-size space shuttle.

ALABAMA ALMANAC

Statehood date and number: December 14, 1819, 22nd

State seal: Adopted 1819; readopted by law in 1939

State flag: Adopted 1895

Geographic center: Chilton, 12 miles (19 km) southwest of Clanton

Total area/rank: 52,419 square miles (135,765 sq km)/30th

Coastline: 53 miles (85 km)

Borders: Mississippi, Tennessee, Georgia, Florida, and the Gulf of Mexico

Latitude and longitude: Alabama is located approximately between 84° 51' and 88° 28' N and 30° 13' and 35° 00' W

Highest/lowest elevation: Cheaha Mountain, 2,407 feet (734 m)/sea level at the Gulf of Mexico

Hottest/coldest temperature: 112° Fahrenheit (44° Celsius) at Centreville on September 5, 1925/–27°F (–33°C) at New Market on January 30, 1966

Land area/rank: 50,744 square miles (131,426 sq km)/28th

Inland water area: 956 square miles (2,476 sq km)

Population/rank (2000 census): 4,447,100/23rd

Population of major cities:
- **Birmingham:** 242,820
- **Mobile:** 198,915
- **Montgomery:** 201,568
- **Huntsville:** 158,216
- **Tuscaloosa:** 77,906

Origin of state name: Alabama was named for the Alabama Indians

State capital: Montgomery

Previous capitals: Huntsville (1819), Cahaba (1820–1826), and Tuscaloosa (1826–1846)

Counties: 67

State government: 35 senators, 105 representatives

Major rivers and lakes: Alabama River, Mobile River, Tombigbee River, Guntersville Lake, and Wheeler Lake

Farm products: Cotton, corn, eggs, milk, oats, peanuts, pecans, potatoes, poultry, soybeans, tobacco, and wheat

Livestock: Broilers, beef cattle

Manufactured products: Aluminum, fertilizer, cast iron, furniture, metal, paper, paint, plastic, steel, rubber, chemicals, textiles, automobiles, and varnish

Mining products: Coal, clay, iron ore, limestone, lumber, marble, natural gas, and petroleum

Fishing products: Bass, bream, buffalo fish, catfish, crabs, croakers, flounder, mackerel, mussels, mullet, oysters, red snapper, and shrimp

Amphibian: Red hills salamander

Bird: Yellowhammer woodpecker

Butterfly: Eastern tiger swallowtail

Drama: *The Miracle Worker* by William Gibson

Flower: Camellia

Freshwater fish: Largemouth bass

Fossil: *Basilosaurus cetoides*

Game bird: Wild turkey

Gem: Star blue quartz

Horse: Racking horse

Insect: Monarch butterfly

Mineral: Hematite, also called red iron ore

Motto: *Audemus Jura Nostra Defendere* (Latin for "We dare defend our rights")

Nicknames: The Heart of Dixie, the Cotton State, the Camellia State, the Yellowhammer State

Nut: Pecan

Quilt: Pine Burr Quilt

Reptile: Alabama red-bellied turtle

Saltwater fish: Fighting tarpon

Shell: Johnstone's junonia

Soil: Bama soil series

Song: "Alabama," words by Julia S. Tutwiler and music by Edna Gockel Gussen

Stone: Marble

Tree: Southern longleaf pine

Wildlife: Alligators, beavers, bobcats, coral snakes, water moccasins, deer, ducks, foxes, geese, minks, opossums, otters, owls, quail, rabbits, raccoons, rattlesnakes, skunks, squirrels, turkeys, turtles, yellowhammer woodpeckers, and other birds

TIMELINE

ALABAMA STATE HISTORY

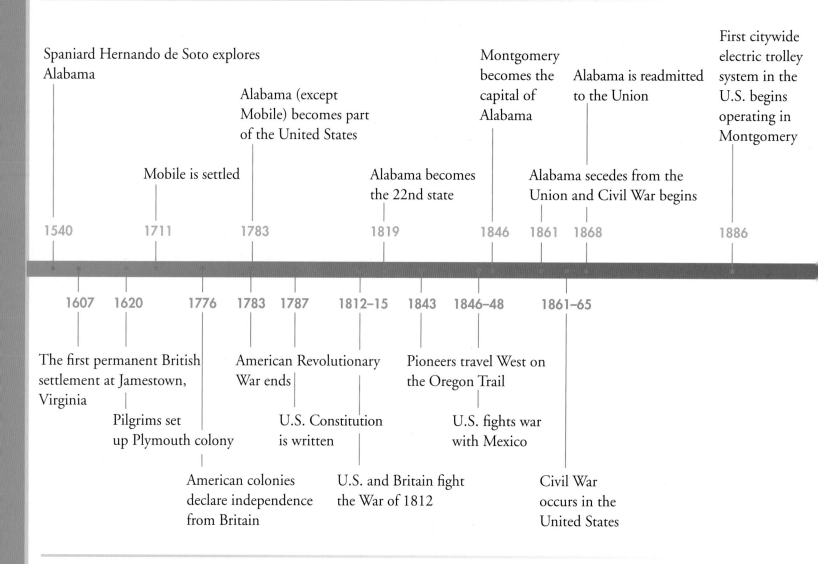

Spaniard Hernando de Soto explores Alabama

Alabama (except Mobile) becomes part of the United States

Montgomery becomes the capital of Alabama

Alabama is readmitted to the Union

First citywide electric trolley system in the U.S. begins operating in Montgomery

Mobile is settled

Alabama becomes the 22nd state

Alabama secedes from the Union and Civil War begins

1540   **1711**   **1783**   **1819**   **1846** **1861** **1868**   **1886**

1607 **1620**   **1776** **1783** **1787**   **1812–15** **1843** **1846–48**   **1861–65**

The first permanent British settlement at Jamestown, Virginia

American Revolutionary War ends

Pioneers travel West on the Oregon Trail

Pilgrims set up Plymouth colony

U.S. Constitution is written

U.S. fights war with Mexico

American colonies declare independence from Britain

U.S. and Britain fight the War of 1812

Civil War occurs in the United States

UNITED STATES HISTORY

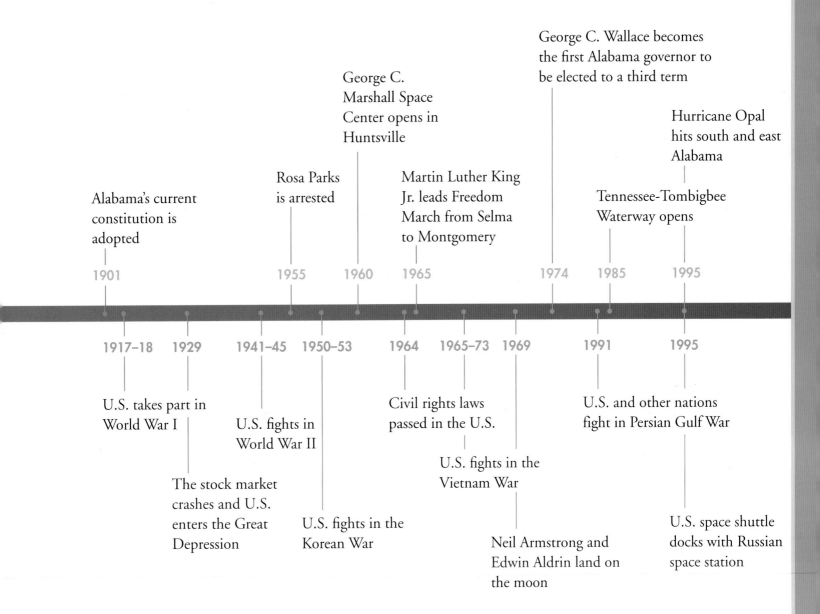

George C. Wallace becomes the first Alabama governor to be elected to a third term

Hurricane Opal hits south and east Alabama

George C. Marshall Space Center opens in Huntsville

Rosa Parks is arrested

Martin Luther King Jr. leads Freedom March from Selma to Montgomery

Tennessee-Tombigbee Waterway opens

Alabama's current constitution is adopted

1901   **1955**   **1960**   **1965**   **1974**   **1985**   **1995**

1917–18   **1929**   **1941–45**   **1950–53**   **1964**   **1965–73**   **1969**   **1991**   **1995**

U.S. takes part in World War I

U.S. fights in World War II

Civil rights laws passed in the U.S.

U.S. and other nations fight in Persian Gulf War

U.S. fights in the Vietnam War

The stock market crashes and U.S. enters the Great Depression

U.S. fights in the Korean War

Neil Armstrong and Edwin Aldrin land on the moon

U.S. space shuttle docks with Russian space station

GALLERY OF FAMOUS ALABAMIANS

Ralph Abernathy

(1926–1990)

Civil rights leader and Baptist minister. In 1968, he led a march on Washington, D.C. as part of the Poor People's Campaign to protest poverty, unemployment, and racial discrimination. Born in Linden.

Tallulah Bankhead

(1903–1968)

Popular film and stage actress who was famous for her sophisticated style and deep voice. Born in Huntsville.

Hugo Black

(1886–1971)

Served as a United States senator (1927–1939) before being appointed Associate Justice of the United States Supreme Court in 1937. Born in Harlan.

Nat "King" Cole

(1919–1965)

Award-winning singer and composer. He won the 1950 Academy Award for his recording of "Mona Lisa," and was the first African-American to host his own television and radio shows. Born in Montgomery.

Helen Keller

(1880–1968)

Author and educator. Deaf and blind from the age of 2, she learned to speak, read, and write with the help of her teacher, Anne Sullivan. In 1904, she graduated with honors from Radcliffe College in Cambridge, Massachusetts. Born in Tuscumbia.

Coretta Scott King

(1927– 2006)

Civil-rights leader and the widow of Dr. Martin Luther King Jr. Born in Heiberger.

Harper Lee

(1926–)

Author of Pulitzer prize-winning novel *To Kill a Mockingbird*, set in a small Alabama town. Published in 1960, it is still one of the best-loved novels in the history of American literature. She lives in Monroeville and New York.

Julia Tutwiler

(1841–1916)

Teacher and advocate for prison reform. In 1898, she forced the entry of women into the University of Alabama. She also established what is today the University of Montevallo. Born in Tuscaloosa.

GLOSSARY

alliance: a uniting of nations, states or other parties with a common interest

assassinated: killed by another person, usually for religious or political reasons

citizen: member of a city, state, or country

civil rights: the right of all citizens to be treated fairly and equally

Confederacy: the new nation formed by a group of eleven southern states (1860–1865) after leaving the United States

export: to send products from one country to another in return for goods, money, or services

integrated: to end racial separation by bringing blacks and whites together

majority: more than half

monument: a building, statue, or place that was built in remembrance of a person or an event

segregation: separating blacks from whites in public places

subtropical: a warm climate

unconstitutional: not in agreement with the United States Constitution

FOR MORE INFORMATION

Web sites

Alabama Department of Archives Webpage for Kids
http://www.archives.state.al.us/kidspage/kids.html
Includes information about Alabama's history, governors, important people, and state symbols.

Alabama.gov
http://www.alabama.gov
Alabama's official website containing links to information about the state government.

Alabama Tourism
http://www.touralabama.org
Information about attractions and destinations throughout Alabama.

Books

George, Linda and Charles George. *The Tuskegee Airmen*. Danbury, CT: Children's Press, 2001.

Greenfield, Eloise. *Rosa Parks*. New York, NY: HarperCollins Children's Books, 1996.

Murphy, Jim. *Boys War: Confederate and Union Soldiers Talk About the Civil War*. New York, NY: Clarion Books, 1993.

Tertius, James de Kay. *Meet Martin Luther King, Jr. (Bullseye Biography)*. New York, NY: Random House, 1994.

Addresses

Alabama Bureau of Tourism & Travel
401 Adams Avenue, Suite 126
P.O. Box 4927
Montgomery, AL 36103-4927

Alabama Department of Archives and History
P.O. Box 300100
624 Washington Avenue
Montgomery, AL 36103-0100
http://www.archives.state.al.us

Governor of Alabama
State Capitol
Room N-104
600 Dexter Avenue
Montgomery, AL 36130
http://www.governor.state.al.us

INDEX

ABOUT THE AUTHOR

Kathy Feeney is a freelance travel writer and the author of more than thirty nonfiction books for children. She received a bachelor's degree in journalism from the University of South Florida and worked as a newspaper reporter for 14 years. She is a member of the Society of Children's Book Writers and Illustrators and the North American Travel Journalists Association. Feeney is the recipient of several awards, including a William Randolph Hearst Award for writing. She lives in Tampa, Florida.

Photographs © 2009: Alabama Bureau of Tourism & Travel: 3 left, 67 (Dan Brothers), 63, 65, 66 (Karim Shamsi Basha); AP Images/Dave Martin: 14; Bud Hunter: 40, 49; Corbis Images: 70 bottom (Tony Arruza), 54 (Richard Cummins), 44 (Kevin Fleming), 7, 62 (Raymond Gehman), 38 (Flip Schulke), 71 bottom left (Tim Thompson), 37 (UPI), 24, 29 top, 56 bottom; Folio, Inc./Jeff Greenberg: cover; Getty Images: 74 bottom right (Archive Photos), 20 (Richard A. Cooke III/Stone), 26, 32, 35, 39 (Hulton Archive), 58 (Keith Wood/Stone); Globe Photos: 55, 56 top; MapQuest.com, Inc.: 70 top left; National Geographic Image Collection/John Schneeberger: 57; North Wind Picture Archives: 12 (Nancy Carter), 19, 21, 22 left, 28, 31; Photo Researchers, NY: 42, 46 background (Bill Aron), 50 (Van Bucher), 52 (Thomas S. England), 41 (Bruce Roberts); Robertstock.com: 9 top (J. Greenberg/Camerique), 4 (F. Sieb), 71 top left; Stock Boston/William Johnson: 16; Stock Montage, Inc.: 22 right, 27, 29 bottom, 33, 64, 74 left, 74 top right; Visuals Unlimited: 70 top right (Scott Berner), 48 (Jeff Greenberg), 71 top right (L. Linkhart), 17 (Ernest Manewal), 3 right, 11 (Erwin C. Nielsen), 9 bottom, 71 bottom right (Glenn M. Oliver), 8, 69 (Chick Piper).